UK Quilters
United by a common thread

N.D.

UK Quilters
United by a common thread

The story of 21st century quilting
as told by over one hundred quilters
from across the United Kingdom

3rd edition
Reproduction of original version

Julie Passey

UK Quilters
United by a common
thread

Copyright © 2016 Dr. Julie Passey

The rights of Dr Julie Passey to be identified
as the author of this work has
been asserted by her in accordance with
the Copyright, Designs and Patents Act 1988

First edition, 2016
Published in a limited edition of one hundred copies
Collated, edited and published by Dr. Julie Passey
ISBN 978-0-9935904-0-5

Second edition (text only), 2019
Published as ebook and paperback
Reformatted and published by Nina Danielsson
Paperback ISBN 978-1-7956-5745-7

Third edition (reproduction of original), 2019
Published as paperback
Reformatted and published by Nina Danielsson
Paperback ISBN 978-1-7957-7818-3

In memory of my first quilt friends
JENNY & GRACE
who opened my eyes to the real
reasons why I quilt

TABLE OF CONTENTS

FOREWORD

To quote Ellen Birdseye Wheaton in her diary written in 1851: "All my scattering moments are taken up with my needle" For me, this quote is very apt! Cloth needle and thimble are the tools that I use virtually every day of my life, and have done for very many years. To be able to immerse oneself in something that brings such personal fulfilment and joy is a real privilege.

I have also had the privilege of being a quilt teacher for almost thirty years, and during that time I have met hundreds of women who have been introduced to the craft. For many, this is the beginning of a totally new life, especially for those who have had serious illness in their lives, or who have been bereaved, and frequently for women who have retired, and suddenly find such enjoyment from the sense of community and friendship that quilting offers. A phrase I have heard frequently is: "I wish I had found this years ago!"

I have worked as a health professional, in hospitals and in the community, and am well aware of the isolation, loneliness, sadness and stresses that many people cope with day in and day out.

For those who are introduced to quilting it can literally be a lifeline. One put her arm around my shoulder recently, and announced; "This lady literally saved my life!" What she meant was that she had signed up for a quilting course that I was teaching, which had changed her world. It opened up new avenues; released talents which had lain dormant, and connected her to a network with creative, exciting and enriching new prospects. It gave her an escape once a week, from a daily routine which was smothering her. Now, she gives talks and sells her work, and she is inspiring a whole new generation.

Many quilters find that this happens for them. The sense of personal fulfilment and creativity gives such joy and is so empowering. A huge amount of funds are raised by quilting groups every year for charities at home and abroad. Such pleasure is gained by "making for giving"! International Community Assist (ICA) is one such charity, based in England. They work in Albania, assisting families who live in desperately poor conditions. One of the ways they are helping is through a project which teaches women sewing skills. This is literally life changing. Many families are being lifted out of poverty, by bringing in a living wage. Women are being employed in local factories or are self-employed. The benefits are numerous. Profits from the sale of this book are very generously being donated to this charity to help them continue their fantastic work.

Stitching can literally transform people's lives, whether by giving solace, extending the hand of friendship and community or by giving a sense of worth. We are so fortunate to be able to share our love of quilting in so many ways.

Di Wells
August 2015

INTRODUCTION

- 2015 -

I'm such a loner! Two years ago I would go for weeks, honest to goodness weeks, without talking to another adult, save the checkout ladies at Tesco ...now I have the group, and lots of friends, and I went to Cornwall on holiday and met loads of them! This group really means a lot to some of us, me for definite.

Two years ago, I dug out some fabric, set up my sewing machine in the lounge and joined an international quilting group on Facebook for inspiration. It was interesting, but it was mostly members from the USA and hard to find UK members to chat to. Another member agreed with me that we needed something specifically for us and I bit the bullet and started UK Quilters United. The group grew rapidly and became such a friendly, happy, encouraging place to show pictures of quilts and ask questions.

With members ranging from complete beginners, to authors and award winners, we see a lot of amazing quilts and someone will always help you out if you need advice. Our main intention is to get people involved and get them together. We have competitions, UKQU project groups, even ribbons to wear to conventions so you can spot and say hello to other members. We put great emphasis on finding our members local groups to join and people to quilt with, spawning many new friendships in real life, not just on Facebook.

It's been an amazing journey so far and there's so much more to go. This isn't just a Facebook group now - it's a community of like-minded women and men of all ages, from every corner of the United Kingdom. All sharing their journeys together.

Juliet Nice,
Co-founder of UK Quilters United

- 2019 -

The original 100 copies of the book, which were collated and printed during 2015 and 2016, have all sold and unfortunately this meant that many of our members (now over 15,000) haven't been able to read all the lovely stories already written by and about UK Quilters United.

At the beginning of 2019, we celebrated five years as an online quilt group and decided it is time to create a new book. We approached Dr. Julie Passey to let her know our plans and to ask if we could share the stories she collated and published. She kindly sent us her files and gave us permission to republish the book.

So far, we have released all the original stories in an ebook for Kindle. Having learnt a bit more about the publishing options on Amazon, we have also released a print on demand version of the ebook. Both of these versions are text only, i.e. there are no images; still they offer an opportunity for everyone to read the lovely stories written by our members. We call both these, the second edition.

Move forward a few weeks, and we created this, the third edition, with the same content as the original book, including almost all original images and the original pattern by AbbieAnne Searle; the layout has changed slightly due to a different page size.

Unfortunately, Julie's selected charity, *International Community Assist*, has ceased to exist, so instead any profits made from the sale of the books (second and third editions), will be used to contribute to UK Quilters United's direct costs.

We are extremely grateful to Julie for allowing us to use her manuscript for a reproduction

We hope that you'll enjoy the stories and are as excited as we are about the second book which should be published later during 2019.

Thank you for your support and hopefully 'see' you in one of our Facebook groups.

Nina Danielsson,
Co-founder of UK Quilters United
www.facebook.com/ukquiltersunited

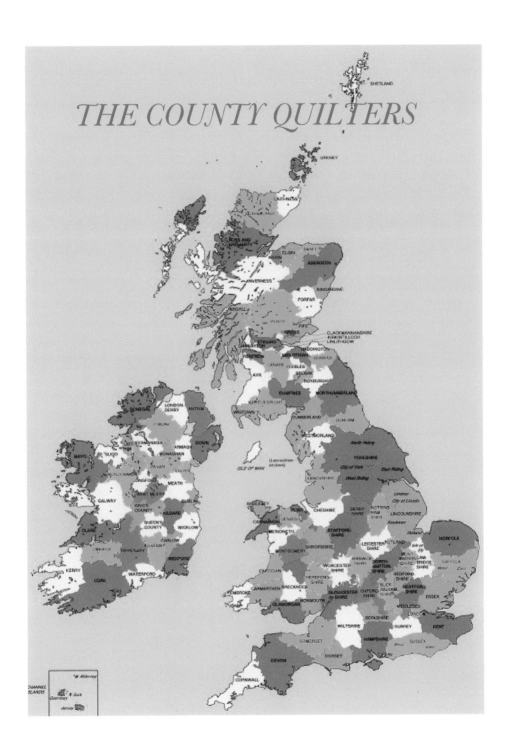

THE COUNTY QUILTERS

A Bedfordshire quilter

Dear Reader,

It began with a simple question: "Don't you think this is pretty?" And from there, my aunt had me. She'd shown me a picture of Robyn Pandolph's Bespoke Blooms, the U.S. queen-size appliqué quilt that would consume my available crafting hours for the next three years. Little did I know when I began it I'd have a chance to move to the country that inspired every block, each named after a lovely part of the UK! Bath, Castle Cary, Porlock, and Wells are just a few, but my favourite was Nunney, pictured here. I used Robyn's Somerset Cottage fabric line and my Aunt Eula did the quilting.

In my family, hand work is seen as a blessing the women passed down. My mom sewed matching outfits for my dolls and me. My mom, sister, aunts, and cousins hold quilting retreats at Grandma Irene's house in Illinois, which is quite the trip now that I live in over here. Sewing relaxes me; keeping my hands busy frees my mind. The creative processes of colour placement, fabric selection, the beautiful hand-dyed batiks and threads...the repeated motion of the needle back and forth through the fabric slowing the pace of an all-too-often frenetically paced modern life...engaging multiple senses brings peace. K.S.

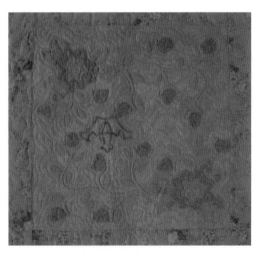

Bespoke Blooms

A Berkshire Quilter

Dear Reader,

I am a wife and full time working mum to two young children living in a village on the edge of Bracknell and during the last year have found a wonderful passion for quilting. I have a close friend who made a quilt for my daughter's christening and I thought it was the most beautiful present because it had been made by her with love and care. Shortly after I was given a sewing machine as a longed for birthday and Christmas present and decided that what I most wanted to do with it was learn how to quilt. The first quilt I ever made was very small and simple, made of 4 blocks, 2 rail fence and 2 four square blocks. This was as a part of a course I took in Exeter, Devon to learn about machine piecing and quilting and because I was staying near the sea I made it from a nautical themed fabric and gave it to my mother in law as a way of say thank you for all the times we stayed in their holiday cottage in the South Hams.

I started to quilt out of a fascination with creating something, but as I learnt it became more than that, the act of being able to complete each little task – planning, buying fabric, pressing, cutting, piecing, pressing again, basting and finally quilting, helped my mind to settle and the weight of whatever was worrying me at the time lifted, bringing a deep sense of calm. The dreaded hand sewing to finish binding the edges of each quilt has now become a stage I look forward to, the simple rhythm of using the needle, while I sit with my husband or listen to music or even sometimes whilst watching a movie – though that has led to stabbing myself with the needle on more than one occasion!

Quilting has helped me when I have been in my worst moments as someone who suffers from depression. Completing just one little stage of the process gives me a sense of satisfaction and a feeling of accomplishment that lifts my day and changes a "blue" outlook to a sunny one. I had thought that quilting would be a hobby for me, but it has become a family obsession, my wonderful husband involved in planning new quilts and providing that extra pair of hands when trying to spray baste a quilt far too large to fit anywhere but the dining room floor. My children are now fascinated by my sewing machine and are learning to quilt with me, giving them a skill I know will mean something to them as they grow.

Chain of adventures for my son

Quilting has also given me some funny moments, such as managing to sew my trousers to an English Paper Pieced hexagon flower. It is also introducing me to a whole new world of generous and supportive friends. I have not come across another hobby where strangers from all over the world are kind and helpful instantly when there is a problem to try to fix, or encouraging and full of needed advice when starting a new project or just trying something new. Social media can be a double edged sword, but the quilting world puts it to a better and more positive use, I love that my Facebook timeline is filled with beautiful quilts every time I look at it – or jokes about fabric stashes! I hope that as this wonderful hobby grows in the UK, more people can come to know the special qualities that quilting can bring to their life. C. B.

The Buckinghamshire Quilters

Dear Reader,

I am the wife of a train driver and have 2 grown up children and a 2 year old grandson. I live in a city called Milton Keynes that is best known for its concrete cows and roundabouts. It was at a mums and tots group that I got into patchwork, the first quilt I made was bad, it was squares and a border. It was just good to think that I had made it.

I love looking at all the different colours and patterns of quilts. I have found that patchwork helps gives me a sense of achievement when I am feeling low due to my illness. I have also made a great group of friends that are always there for each other to give support at good times and bad ones. I am blessed to have them and my patchwork which I would be lost without.

I love it when I go into my sewing room and get all my books and material out and decide what I am going to make .I can lose myself up in my room for hours, just planning and laying my material out. I have done some appliqué and really enjoyed it, so going to try some more and be a bit more adventurous with the patterns and not be afraid to experiment with shapes, colours and materials. I think without my patchwork I would have gone mad.

I would say to anyone who is thinking of taking up patch work to give it a go and be surprised at what you can achieve and the friends you will make along the way. A.P.

Night owl by the light of the silvery moon. My first competition piece and I won the long arm machine quilting award at Sandown, wholecloth on Robert Kaufman radiance fabric, glide thread by Superior Threads. J.B.

The Cambridge Quilters

Dear Reader,

I am a wife and mother of two grown up children and I have a passion for quilting. I live in a small town in rural Cambridgeshire, near the Lincolnshire and Rutland borders I've been quilting for three years, and now quilt daily. The first quilt I ever made was of fabric purchased whilst on holiday in the USA, including fabric from an Amish lady in Lancaster. It was a memory quilt / sample quilt, it took me ages to complete ... and I loved it!

I took up quilting to pass the time after being made redundant and it has taken over. I go to two different quilt groups and will not make any other arrangements on those days so I don't miss the group. I love making and gifting quilts to family and friends, especially new arrivals. These quilts are always sewn with much happiness at the thought of a little one snuggled under my stitches and fabric.

In our group we have just all done a mystery quilt over 6 months. It was a challenge and with plenty of unpicking, naughty words and trying to stretch the fabric with an iron to make the blocks the right size! I began to call mine not a mystery quilt, but a miracle quilt, 'cos it would be a miracle if I ever finished it. I am pleased to say the quilt is now on my spare bed and looks amazing.

I have made some lovely friends through the groups and also through UKQU, one lady actually went and got some more fabric for me, as she lived near to the shop I had brought it from, and posted it as a gift to me. All from a lovely lady I had only chatted to on the internet.

I can say I am a very happy quilter, and on that note, I have a quilt to finish, as a gift for a newborn little lady. J.O.

My first quilt, made with my late husband's shirts. L.M.

The Cheshire Quilters

Dear Reader,

I'm a wife and aunty / great aunty to 11 nieces, nephews, great nieces and great nephews. I live in a railway town in Cheshire and spent 35 years of my working life working for the railway.

I've been sewing for most of my life, having been given scraps of fabric to play with when my brother was a baby, as it kept me out of mischief. I had the best dressed Sindy doll in the area.

Over the last 45+ years I have turned my hand to most aspects of sewing. Since losing my mum who was my inspiration, I have taken my passion for sewing to new levels and have now turned to quilting. Despite having planned many quilts on graph paper (I find the planning quite therapeutic and take my sketchbook with me on long train journeys), so far I have only tackled small projects.

I am now planning my first big quilt, in grey and cream fabric ~ it won't be anything overly complicated but it will be mine and something that I will be extremely proud of. I will no doubt bore friends and family to death with the story of it.

My new found love for quilting has brought me into contact with some inspirational people and has filled my life and house with fabric, some of which is far too nice to cut into, which means I have to buy two lots of each… one to use and one to caress. S.B.

Tulips
My second quilt – I love applique! E.W.

A Cornish Quilter

Dear Reader,

I am a wife and full time reception class teacher who has found that I love to quilt. I live just outside the busy coastal town of Falmouth. My first attempt at quilting was over thirty years ago when I began to (badly) piece together hexagons I had cut out of scraps of fabric, however at that stage I was too impatient and it ended up as a floor cushion!

Looking back I think I recall seeing my aunty working on some patchwork and thinking that it looked so pretty. I tried many crafts, but always came back to fabric and threads. I joined a creative embroidery group and was inspired to try new techniques, one of which was machine embroidery...I was hooked!

I showed off my pieces to my work colleagues and found someone else with the same interests, we began to go to various workshops and eventually found ourselves working on the Leeds Tapestry, with Paddy Killer. I later became involved in a tapestry for the village and the lady who's house we used to have the meetings at had some wonderful quilts hanging up on her wall that I so admired.

Moving to Cornwall I found I was in a house with a big wall that just needed filling, one jelly roll later and a log cabin quilt was made. Through the purchasing of quilting kits, books, magazines, the internet and the rather wonderful UKQU Facebook group, I have made quite a few more and regard myself now as a quilter!

Quilting to me is a way of relaxing and de-stressing, just letting your mind wander as you cut and sew and create something beautiful. I like to sit and stroke my fabrics and to me a visit to a quilting shop is a chance to admire, covert and plan projects.

Quilting takes over your life (and your house) and I have found that I like to have a couple of projects on the go, one for the machine, which sits proudly on my kitchen table, and one to do by hand, while watching the TV.

I have one "real" quilty friend but through UKQU, Facebook and Instagram, I have discovered a whole new world of quilting friends. The inspiration, encouragement and support I receive from these has opened up a whole new world for me and one that I treasure.

For any would-be-quilters, give it a go, for you might find your life transformed! S.W.

A County Durham Quilter

Dear Reader,

Currently living in a former pit village in County Durham, I'm grandma to beautiful 7 year old twin girls. I've only been quilting for two years, but am introducing the girls to it when they visit.

I was first introduced to patchwork and quilting five years ago, but didn't get into it at that time. With a stressful job, living in a different area, I was looking for something to help me unwind. A free gift on the cover of a quilting magazine led me to buy the magazine and start exploring this craft. I find it very therapeutic, relaxing after a stressful day. I'm also taken out of my comfort zone when I participate in swaps, making for others according to their wishes and seeing how others interpret my wishes in fabric. Learning new techniques also keeps my mind active.

Although I do both machine and hand stitching, my current favourite technique is English Paper Piecing. Because this is hand sewn it is portable and can be done anywhere. After work I can sit in front of the TV and sew for hours.

I love the way patchwork and quilting has shown me new ways to relax creatively, introduced me to many new friends, and taught me not to be too hard on myself.

There is something for everyone in the world of patchwork and quilting, from the traditional to the contemporary. We need to explore and experiment with new techniques while not abandoning our traditions, encouraging others to try their hand at this craft. L.D.

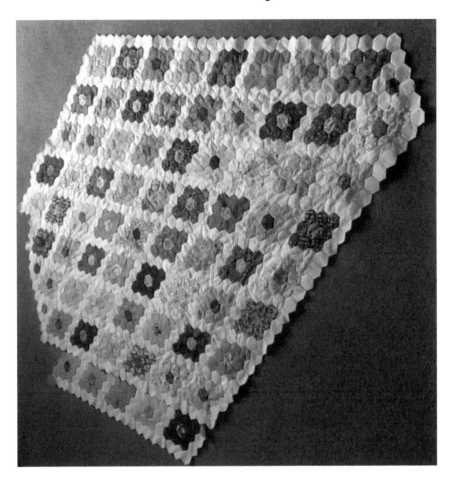

The Cumbrian Quilters

Dear Reader,

I am a mother of two grown up sons and I have a huge passion for patchwork and quilting. I am fairly new to all things sewing and was prompted to take up a new hobby after recent health issues left me disabled. Over the years I have tried many crafts, but none have grabbed me like patchwork and quilting.

I love a challenge and created my first piece using paper piecing in a block pattern. I spend a lot of time using clothes and fabric items that are of no use to people, perhaps due to holes etc. I love creating new things from old and find patchwork very therapeutic.

The main thing I have learnt through my discovery of patchwork and quilting is...there are no mistakes, just lessons I am learning on this exciting journey.   M.D.

A 'stack the deck' quilt made with fat quarters. S.R.

The Derbyshire Quilters

Dear Reader,

I am a mother of two grown daughters and a grandmother of two small grandchildren. I live in a small rural village in Derbyshire. My daughter and I only started patchwork and quilting 3months ago, following a visit to the Uttoxeter show, where we were so impressed, we had to have a go.

The first quilt I made was a small cot quilt made from a fat quarter bundle. I didn't know if I had made it right, but it looked ok and I was quite impressed with the result. I wasn't sure what I was going to do with it. I joined a couple of Facebook groups and in one of them a lady was asking for quilts to be donated to the disaster in Nepal, so I just knew this was where my little quilt needed to go.

Since then I have made a couple of memory quilts, the first made with my granddaughter's baby clothes and the second for my other daughter, who lost her beloved dog in May. I made her a special quilt with all the dogs names on that she and my son in law had owned.

I am now trying English paper piecing, making hexagon flowers, which through another Facebook page, I am swapping all over the world. This will make a beautiful friendship quilt when it's finished. I have made some nice friends in this wonderful pastime.

My biggest ambition though, is to put our family tree on a quilt. I just have to figure out the best design, but it will happen, as quilting and patchwork has become a bit of an obsession! S.B.

For future generations
My first quilt - hoping it'll become a family heirloom. L.B

The Devon Quilters

Dear Reader,

I live in the south west of England and I am in my early 60's. I am widowed and a mother, grandmother and great grandmother and wish I had found this lovely hobby of patchwork and quilting earlier in my life.

I started sewing clothes for my dolls at a very early age and was given a battery operated sewing machine one Christmas.

I continued to make clothes for all the family, until my lovely other half died and 18 months later my youngest child was found dead at the age of 29.

Falling Back
Currently on tour until 2016 with Grovesnor Shows. G.D.

I needed something to fill my head and my time, to stop me thinking so much of my losses. It was then I found an advert in the local paper for beginners P & Q classes and went along to have ago. That was 5 years ago and I am still enjoying it.

Instead of clothes, the family are now getting quilts, which will last long after I am no longer here. I have also started showing a couple of friends how to enjoy this lovely hobby. M.J.

Ho, Ho, Ho! K.B.

The Dorset Quilters

Dear Reader,

My quilting journey started just after being off work for an extended period, due to ill health. Having taken up other crafts that had lain dormant for many years, which I have given as presents, I turned my hand to patchwork and quilting this year.

By the way, I am 56 years old so you are never too old to start!

My first attempt was a quilt using a sewing machine. I can recommend starting with a machine made quilt, as they grow so quickly and so does your enthusiasm. Since then I have made a number of quilts for a girl at works little girls, as she was on a tight budget and I thought they would be nice. She was delighted to receive these gifts.

I've just done an heirloom quilt for my son's wedding. I have by no means mastered all the techniques, or even the language. I have now started a hand sewn quilt in hexagons, which I plan to hand quilt. This is great to put in a tin in your handbag, so you can take a small part with you on journeys.

I hope you will join us on this journey and create some wonderful items that will become the heirlooms of the future. C.H. (Newbie quilter).

Arbour of our love H.S.

An Essex Quilter

Dear Reader,

I live near Basildon, Essex with my husband and our two dogs. I have a son and a daughter who have now flown the nest. I am a primary school teacher with a passion for Early Years. My other passion is, of course, patchwork and quilting. I have sewn since I was a child, but have only been quilting for about a year. It happened quite by accident really. I joined a Facebook fabric swapping group and one of the lovely ladies I made a swap with is an avid, and very talented, quilter. Well, we got chatting and the next thing I knew, I was making a quilt!

For my most recent quilt I decided to make it truly unique by dying my own fabric (see photo). The beauty of this was, as I ran out of a particular colour, I just put my rubber gloves on and got the dyes out! I can't wait to give this quilt to my son and his girlfriend for Christmas.

As my kids have left home I have spare rooms, one of which has become my beloved sewing room. I pop the radio on, light a scented candle and I'm in quilting heaven. Most of my quilted projects, which are quite often bags (I'm a bit of a bag lady!) I make as gifts, so not only do I sew for my own pleasure, but for the pleasure of friends and family.

As I sign off, my words of advice to anybody wishing to join me on this wonderful journey of patchwork and quilting are – equip yourself with the basic essential tools; self-healing cutting mat, rotary cutter and quilting ruler; browse the web, or preferably a 'real-life' fabric shop, for fabrics that scream out to be stroked, and get creating.

Most of all, have fun and remember, there are no such thing as quilting police! L.G.

The Gloucestershire Quilters

Dear Reader,

I am a wife and mother of two grown up children and I have a passion for quilting. I live in a small town in rural Gloucestershire and have been quilting for thirty five years. The first quilt I ever made was of English paper pieced hexagons (EPP). It used every scrap of fabric I owned, looked terrible, took me forever to complete ... and I absolutely loved it!

I don't think it is exaggerating to say that quilting has been my lifeline on more than one occasion. Whatever the world has thrown at me has been sewn into a quilt, every emotion possible has found its way into the designs, stitches, blocks and patterns that make up the sum total of my work. Above all, it gives me a time to think; untangling threads, choosing colours, making plans, all offer a measure of control and a way to make sense of the world - or at least a chance to come to terms with it.

Quilting can be very sociable, it has given me some of my best and truest friends. Despite this, my favourite times are when I am lost in my own space. I love to hand quilt because it can be done 'any time, any place, anywhere'. Early in the morning, it energises me and bring a sense of purpose to a day, in the evening it unwinds my mind and brings a deep sense of calm.

I hope that in the future, more people can come to know the special qualities that quilting can bring to their life. Qualities above and beyond the obvious benefits of discovering a new skill, extending our knowledge of other cultures, finding friendship in the most unlikely places...less obvious bonuses such as inner peace, self-esteem and the satisfaction of continuing a tradition of creating something beautiful and useful that will long outlive us. J.P.

Falling Leaves
My first quilt, a nine patch. I'd been quilting nine months when I completed this. J.W.

The Hampshire Quilters

Dear Reader,

I am a middle aged quilter, with a husband of 35 years and two sons in their early twenties. We live in a picturesque town in southern Hampshire and I am at home with severe fibromyalgia and M.E. which can be a bit bleak – although luckily my town does have a good quilt shop.

I made my first cot quilt when I was expecting my eldest son, but my passion for quilting started after a visit to the American Museum near Bath. We only went one day because it was on the route home from grandparents in Bristol, but their quilts were fabulous – this was before the internet, probably late 70s. Since then, I have made many quilts, often as presents for family, and sometimes just for the sheer joy of the fabrics.

I find that these days my quilting activities are especially important because it takes my mind away from the pain and into a world of colour and texture and focuses on something lovely and creative. I can always find another reason to quilt, thus planning for a future.

My quilts are usually triggered by a photo, or an image, or a shape in the sand or whatever, where the colours are beautiful, although not necessarily to anyone else. I ALWAYS carry a camera with me, thank goodness for smart phones! Finding the colours and playing with the quilting patterns are just two small parts of the quilting that I love. I had lessons from the late June Thorpe, who you might have met, and her way of looking at the subject transformed my quilting completely.

Sometimes there are downsides to quilting, no, not having to buy fabrics, or threads or batting etc, but maybe sitting too long at the sewing machine, too late into the night. Also, knowing when it is finished and mostly having the confidence to show someone, especially if you are doing it for someone else.

My advice for any quilter is to have a go at something small and finish it. That way you don't get bogged down and lose confidence. It is a joyful, fun thing and if it isn't quite straight, or has a hole in it, so what? Put a patch over it and say it was meant to be there! Secondly, don't struggle on your own, there are many quilters hiding in the area, just ask in the local shop, or join an internet group and make new friends who will always want to help and praise what you are doing. S.L.

My first quilt, made for my wonderful mother-in-law. D.L.B.

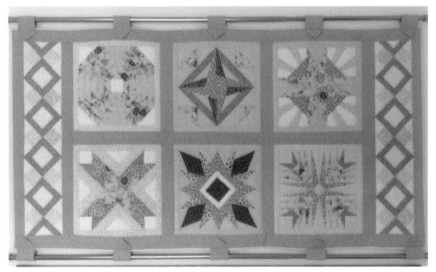

Pinky J.C.

The Herefordshire Quilters

Dear Reader,

My home is a 500 year old, thatched cottage in a village. It is filled with fabrics! I am in my mid-70s, but inside I am still 35. At that time, I worked as a costume designer in TV, and I made my first quilt on location at Elstree Studios. We were making a TV drama on what later became the set for Eastenders. Cold, bored and huddled round a tiny stove in the wardrobe hut, one of the actors asked if I could make quilts. I couldn't, but I found a book, bought a hexie template from the Needlewoman shop in Regent Street and we began. We used old scripts for the acking papers and any scrap of fabric that came to hand. Of course, we made all the usual mistakes, mixed fabrics, over large stitches etc....but I still have that quilt!

My next quilt was made whilst working for the BBC on Penmarric in Cornwall. I started it to amuse several children on the shoot, including Patsy Kensit, who loved to sort out the fabrics for me. By then I knew to only use cottons and it was mostly Tana Lawn. This quilt still lies across the foot of my bed.

In my mid 50s I worked in both sales and interior design for a well-known house builder. I think it was here that my love of quilting was rekindled. It passed the long hours stuck in a sales office and proved a brilliant icebreaker when customers did come in. After that I was hooked, and I worked on alone until the last decade. I now belong to a quilt group, with access to fantastic speakers and other quilters on a regular basis, so my quilt life has expanded in leaps and bounds. It is encouraging to know how many young people are joining, stretching the boundaries with new ideas. I have met new techniques and ideas and been pushed to experiment with embroidery and new designs. I've been endlessly inspired by others' work and now give my own talks about my life in quilts, expanding the craft further. I love it when someone tells me I have inspired them to have a go.

I teach one group and am about to open another. We quilt for church fundraising, families and friends. People ask where I find the time, but if you want it badly enough, you will find it. I quilt and sew in the evenings, in front of the TV. I am adept at listening whilst watching just enough to get the gist of a programme and quilting is great when my husband is watching sport!

I simply find it relaxing and there is nothing better on a cold night in a draughty cottage than being wrapped in a quilt while you hand stitch it. Give it a try, you will never regret it. A.S.

Designed by me and quilted with my quilt class. A.S.

The Hertfordshire Quilters

Dear Reader,

I have been married 44 years, have a son, daughter and 5 lovely grandchildren. My mum and nan taught me how to sew, starting with dolls clothes at the age of 5.

The first thing I did when I started work was to buy my own sewing machine, which meant I could make clothes and later curtains for my home. Patchwork was introduced to me when I was in my late 30's by a neighbour and meant cardboard shapes drawn round with pencil, cut with scissors and sewn by hand, how things have changed!

Patchwork has brought me a wide friendship through groups, The Quilters Guild and now the internet, or more specifically, Facebook groups. Patchwork is my stress buster, it calms me and there is something beautiful at the end of the process. I have started to teach my grandchildren how to sew, the boys like it more than the girls at present.

My favourite quilts are scrap ones, or foundation pieced for the accuracy, and I like making for voluntary organisations: Project Linus and Quilts4London and now items for sale at the charity shops. I'm lucky enough to have my own sewing room, where I can create and make as much mess as possible.

If you are thinking of diving into the world of Patchwork and Quilting, just do it! Join a group, or visit several, to find one that suits you. Have fun and don't worry if your points don't at first join up, you will have achieved a great deal and the person who receives it will love it, because you thought of them.

Welcome to my world or fabric and fun! I.H.

A.S.

An Isle of Wight Quilter

Dear Reader,

I was born in Dundee in 1946, my mother is a Scot, my father was English and I was brought up in southern England. I trained as a nurse, qualifying as an RGN in 1968. I am married with 4 grown up children and 10 grandchildren, ranging from 5 – 23, and a great grandson aged 3. In my forties, I retrained as an adult teacher, teaching child development until I retired to France when I was 58.

When I was 12, we moved into a brand new school with a purpose built housecraft unit, where we were taught to cook, sew, do cleaning and ironing!!!! I was never very interested in sewing and was once caught reading my magazine "Bunty" under the desk. The first thing I made was an apron (to wear in my cooking lessons), then I made a blouse with inset sleeves. I also made a peg bag and a felt flower brooch, as a gift for Mother's Day. As a teenager, my friend and I made a mini shift dress in bright orange and green and I made myself a purple, circular ice-skating skirt. I always felt that I was no good at sewing, so I didn't bother after this, preferring cooking instead.

When I first came to Brittany, I met a lady who introduced me to a sewing group of ex-pat women. At that first meeting I had nothing to take with me, so I borrowed some embroidery thread and Aida from my eldest granddaughter, who was interested in cross stitch. I found a sewing needle and popped it all into a brown paper bag! Despite my meagre notions (see, I learnt new words), the group were very welcoming and very helpful. We met monthly, but my friend was keen to learn patchwork and I agreed to tag along too, as one of the ladies, who had done a course in the UK, agreed to teach us at weekly sessions. Well that was it, I was hooked.

At first I did English Paper Piecing and then bought myself an electric sewing machine, on offer in the "Good Housekeeping" magazine - it still serves me well! To date, I have made lap/cuddly quilts for all of my 11 grandchildren (and one for hubby too, who complained that he hadn't got one). I have also made some for Bristol Children's Hospital. I have made numerous bags and other gifts for Christmas. I also made a tote bag, for carrying all the other bags/pouches that I have made to take all my bits and pieces to the sewing group. We still laugh about my first visit with the brown paper bag.

My message to you dear reader is, you are never too old to learn a new skill. Patchwork and quilting has brought me lifelong friends, who share a love of creating and expressing ourselves in a way I would never have thought possible as a teenager who hated sewing. M.N.

First jelly roll quilt, made 3 years ago for my great-grandson Calvin.
He arrived early, so I had to complete it in record time as it was a gift for his birth.

The Kentish Quilters

Dear Reader,

I am retired after 25 years with the NHS and live with my husband in a small town in Kent, on the very outer edge of Greater London. I fell into quilting about 30 years ago, quite accidentally, having intended to enrol for upholstery classes at our local Adult Education Centre. This class was oversubscribed and my friend and I, being adamant we weren't going to give up a child free evening once a week, decided patchwork and quilting sounded an interesting alternative.

Little did we know this was the first step in an all-consuming hobby, which has brought us so many friends and passed many happy hours, stroking fabric and pondering on the best way to use it.

We were incredibly fortunate to have two absolutely inspirational teachers for those first few years.

In our first year they taught us a new technique every single week and I still have my folder with all their beautiful hand written instructions and the small sample of each technique.

In our second year we completed a sampler quilt, with 25 different blocks, and fell into quite a routine, with the Thursday evening class spent drawing the block and choosing fabrics.

On a Friday I would make the templates and cut out all the fabric and spend Saturday making the block. Sunday through to Thursday was spent hand quilting the block and so on and so on.

I began to resent invitations for the weekend as it upset my quilting schedule! The feeling at the end of the year when all 25 blocks were assembled and quilted was almost indescribable, as none of us had actually believed we would be able to do it.

All these years later, a small group of the original evening class still meet on a weekly basis and we have shared so much over the years - expertise, ideas, fabric, wine, tea, coffee and cake (surely that's in the rules....). They have been an incredible support network, both emotionally and practically, as we have each faced different challenges in life. We have also joined a local quilting group, where there is always something new to learn.

I have been lucky enough to have done a lot of travelling and have met up with quilters in all corners of the world and even attended a quilting picnic in Australia.

Quilters are a wonderful, generous, funny and entertaining breed, who are rarely judgemental and appreciate the efforts of those less skilled, whilst admiring the truly awesome work done by the experts. This is what makes it such a special family and I am so pleased that upholstery class was oversubscribed. G. F.

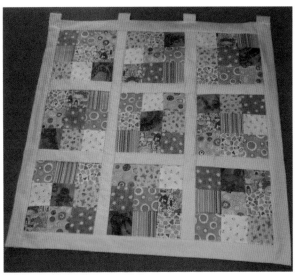

Sudoku in patchwork my first quilt, from a course at my daughter's school. C.J.

For my Emo from a free pattern by Bonnie Hunter. K.H.

The Lancashire Quilters

Dear Reader,

I am married with two children, both of whom are away at university. I live in Liverpool. I am 49 and am semi-retired – just work 3 days a week now, whilst I wind down towards retirement.

I have always sewn since I was a child, but around 3 years ago decided that I wanted to make a patchwork quilt. I had had shop bought ones, but felt that I wanted one that I had made with my own hands. The first one was very simple and since then I've been teaching myself from books and the more I learn the harder it gets! But I love learning new skills. I also find it's time for me to be creative and enjoy creating for pleasure.

Up until 2 years ago I worked full time from home, since going "in house" on a part time basis, my previous home office is redundant. It has now been reclassified as a sewing room and the shelves previously filled with file and reference books now hold material, magazines, craft books. My 2 non-work days are now "sewing" days without feeling guilty.

Quilting offers time for me, without being answerable and responsible for others. I make purely for self-indulgent reasons and all the quilts I make are gifted to family. I want to keep learning, but not in an academic way and this fulfils the brief beautifully.

Enjoy every stitch, make time for yourself and don't fret over tiny mistakes, no-one else will ever notice, but above all …Enjoy! P.F.

My first quilt, a play mat for a new grandson. P.L.

A Leicestershire Quilter

Dear Reader,

I am 59 years old, work full time at a local FE College, am married with grown up children and lots of grandchildren.

It seems a long time ago that I started my first quilt. My daughter was just about a year old; I went along to an adult education class to learn how to make 'American Patchwork' which had piqued my interest. At school I had never been any good at sewing – the teacher had even suggested that I concentrate on some other subject and leave her class…However, I had taught myself to sew the odd dress for myself and my little daughter and was interested to know about patchwork. I loved the names and stories behind the traditional blocks – Bears Paw, Jacobs Ladder, Drunkards Path, Grandmother's Fan and my personal favourite: Log Cabin. My first full sized quilt was a Log Cabin pattern. My 'equipment' at that time was a wooden ruler, a pencil, scissors and a sewing machine. I used to make templates out of cardboard.

So, 34 years on, I have made dozens of quilts in the intervening years, most of which have made their way to friends and family (I especially love making quilts for our grandchildren to cuddle with) – and still love the traditional blocks which drew me to the art in the first place. I love to see the blocks interweave with each other and make secondary patterns. My collection of quilting 'essentials' has grown to include Perspex quilters rulers in various sizes and shapes, rotary cutter, cutting mats, three sewing machines, countless books and magazines and an ever growing stash of fabric. For a long time, I was a 'lone quilter' – I didn't know anyone else who had a similar hobby. And then my friend asked if I would make her a quilt. No, I said, but I will help you make your own. Now I have a quilting buddy – and have found a number of other friends through on-line groups. I have found quilters to be friendly, helpful, inspiring and incredibly generous with their time, expertise and knowledge.

I find peace and satisfaction in making quilts and other quilted objects such as bags and wall hangings. My favourite item is always the one I am working on. If you decide to take up this fascinating pastime – be warned that it is addictive, but you will be part of an ever growing movement of people who are custodians of long-held traditions, imaginative artists and designers propelling patchwork and quilting into the future. I hope you enjoy every piece of patchwork quilting you undertake from the first to the hundred and first. **J.C.**

My first quilt – Log Cabin.

The Lincolnshire Quilters

Dear Reader,

I am a fabricaholic! I have been a 'Lincolnshire Yellowbelly' all my life, and live in a small village next to the River Trent. I have two lovely children and a fabulous grandson. My husband was diagnosed with leukemia earlier this year, so we are facing his challenges together. Quilting is my escape.

What got me started? My best mate bullied me into it really. I have always enjoyed creative activity, and when my kids were young I made their clothes (and mine) plus tried tapestry, embroidery and other handicrafts. But then I returned to work and the machine was put away. So I wanted a lovely quilt like the ones my best mate was making. 'Oh no', she said, 'make your own'. And suddenly we were at a quilt show in Harrogate and I learnt the therapeutic art of stroking fabric. A fabricaholic was born.

The little box of fabric I began with has rapidly grown to populate my small bedroom and is in danger of escaping if I am not careful. I love patchwork. Not so keen on the quilting, I must admit. Piecing the patterns is so satisfying, but no quilt police please - my points often slip and the quilts are rarely square.

My son has my first quilt, a Lintott Tumbling Triangles, in an antique looking Moda fabric (I can't recall the fabric pattern now) and a second red, random patterned one. He would take them all if I allowed him to! My daughter has several smaller quilts for our grandson to crawl about on and is asking for a larger one now. My latest quilt was made for my poorly husband out of 6 fabulous fat quarters of Magee Donegal Tweed and Alexander Henry Nude Ladies. There's a crazy patch of Japanese scraps waiting for quilting too.

There are always quilts on the go, I make little baby quilts for our local NICU because I can – no other reason. My friend and I collate the baby quilts for distribution. I make Fidget Quilts for a group down in Bournemouth now and then – again because I can. Fidget Quilts are so much fun! It's fantastic how generous folk are – and it's all down to UK Quilters United Facebook Group too.

Why do I do it? Because I can. I can't put a reason to it. I just do. It occupies my mind and drives out the worries of everything. I would say to anyone thinking of quilting: Take yourself off to a fabric show, or shop, and browse the fabrics. Feel the joy of pristine, clean fabric under your fingers. Start simple, and don't worry about the end results. Join the UK Quilters United Facebook Group – what a fantastic set of quilty folk. Just enjoy! S.P.

Pond themed quilt for my husband. J.C.

The London Quilters

Dear Reader,

I have two grown up daughters and a lovely 3 year old granddaughter. I live in London, I was born here and have never lived anywhere else. I have been quilting for three years now. I took up quilting with a friend and we have learnt together.

I love visiting the shows and buying kits, but have also done my own designs. Last year we decided to take up an adult education class in patchwork and quilting, to learn techniques. The ladies in the group are lovely and very friendly and we are learning a lot from our fabulous tutor. We have signed up for another term and can't wait to start.

The reason I started quilting was because my father was suffering from dementia and I found it very difficult to see him mentally and physically deteriorate every day. It has also been very difficult and upsetting to deal with my mother's grief as she looked after my dad. Sadly, he had to go into a care home and spent two years there before passing away last year. I can honestly say that quilting has helped me so much to deal with my grief and has kept me sane. I feel without it I could well have had a breakdown over what we have been through. The whole process of starting a quilt, choosing fabrics, measuring and cutting is so therapeutic. To see the end result makes me so proud of what I have achieved, as I am not an artistic person.

My friend and I are making fidget quilts for dementia patients and that we have joined a quilting group that meets once a month. Lovely friendly group that is very welcoming and as well as making Linus quilts the ladies there are also starting to make fidget quilts.

I have converted our box room into a sewing room and it is my haven. I listen to the radio whilst I am sewing and find it very soothing. I have made some small quilts for my granddaughter and have really enjoyed doing appliqué. I have also done a table runner and red work Christmas bunting. I plan to make a large quilt next using, all the different techniques that we are learning and am looking forward to choosing the fabrics.

What I would wish for a would-be quilter is that if you have any problems in your life, it helps you through the difficult times as much as it has helped me. J.L.

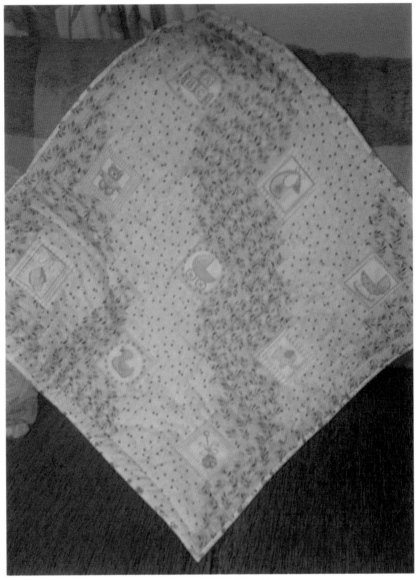

Pram quilt for my niece. R.B.

A Middlesex Quilter

Dear Reader,

I am 46 and live with my cat in my studio flat. It has a dedicated sewing area – which is growing year on year. I've been sewing for as long as I can remember, I embroidered for years and then about 10 years ago I got a machine. I started out with two fabrics that I ordered on line to make a little bag. It had eight squares in it, four each side, lined with the material from an old skirt that no longer fit and the strap also made from the skirt and I absolutely adored it, I still have the bag. I then decided to make my mum a hexagon English paper pieced quilt, which was eventually finished about five years later, but in the meantime I sewed like a demon! I think to date I've made over 60 quilts, various bags, cushions covers, wall hangings and floor cushions.

My favourite sewing time is Saturday morning. I wake up with my creativity just bursting to get out, I have so many ideas of what I want to make. I sew every day; generally evenings are two hours on the machine, then some hand sewing. One of my hand sewing projects always comes away with me.

If I've had a particularly stressful day, I come home and take a drawer of fabric out, tip it up on the table and unfold it, iron it and re-fold and it just takes the stresses away. I think for me it's seeing that bit of fabric and the possibilities that lie within it.

The friends I have made through patchwork and quilting are just great; we do share a laugh over our love of fabric/stash/hoard. I have started a sewing group at my church which now has six members and it is really fulfilling to be able to pass my skills along. My favourite block has to be log cabin, there are so many variations to make, with both the layout and colours and I've made four so far.

My hope for a new patchwork quilter is that they'll find the joy in sewing that I have and make some amazing friends along what I can only call one heck of a journey. J.N.

For the love of scraps

The Norfolk Quilters

Dear Reader,

I have always sewn, my mother taught me when I was very small. We used her old electric Singer that she'd purchased when she knew she was expecting me, in 1951. I enjoyed needlework at school and I spent a lot of time sitting on the front doorstep, embroidering, in my free time.

I was looking for a challenge, something that I would find absorbing and keep me occupied after we lost our son in a road accident in 2013, and began a free machine embroidery course. It wasn't until the following year, when I spotted a beautiful quilt design in a magazine that I took up patchwork and quilting. I loved the colours and way the pieces interlocked to make a pattern. I set off for the local shop almost immediately and selected a range of gorgeous batiks.

It took me several months to complete that quilt, as I kept starting others. I find the different styles and piecing methods fascinating. It's amazing what can be achieved; give a group of patchworkers a vague brief and similar fabrics and they will all produce entirely different results. The other reason the quilt took a long time was that I was afraid to quilt it, in case I messed it up. Then I read a piece by an expert quilter who said it is better that a quilt is inexpertly quilted and used, rather than left in a cupboard.

I enjoy the whole process of patchwork; design, selecting the fabrics, cutting, stitching, layering and quilting. My house isn't as pristine as it used to be and there are always threads lying around, but I'm happier and more able to cope with what life throws at me. I also like that nothing gets wasted, even the tiniest scraps of fabric can be used in something, and that with every seam I sew, my skills improve. I have met a whole new circle of patchworking friends to have fun with, too. Patchwork isn't just a hobby, it's a way of life. B.H.

Machine pieced and in the process of being hand quilted. The inspiration for this quilt came after visiting an ice bar in Austria, lit with different coloured lights. S.R.

The Northamptonshire Quilters

Dear Reader,

I live in a small village in South Northamptonshire. I have lived here since getting married way back in 1979 so you can have a guess how old I am. I only started this quilting lark 2 years ago. A friend of mine was throwing out a 1950's Jones sewing machine and asked if I wanted it. Well, it sat on the dining room floor being moved about when it was in the way till last spring, when my peg bag broke. I thought to myself, I know I have some bits of upholstery fabric under the stairs from when my husband recovered the kitchen chairs, I will have a go at stitching a new bag. It worked a treat, the old Jones sang like a songbird and I soon had a peg bag with an elasticated drawstring top. Pleased as punch, I looked on you tube for different tutorials, discovered Missouri star quilting and away I went. I was soon buying charm packs, layer cakes and different pieces of beautiful fabric from online shops and with the help of you tube, I made my very first table runner, which still sits proudly on my dining room dresser.

One day in early July a friend called in and laughed at me with my sewing machine. Bearing in mind I never sew, the sight of me merrily stitching away must have come as a rare shock. So, she says, did I know there was a fabric shop in her village, who not only sold beautiful fabrics but also held lessons and workshops? The village is Weedon and the shop is The Bramble Patch.

From there my life blossomed! I signed up for a 3 day beginner's course and I loved every day of stitching. Next I joined a weekly class. Such total joy! I do a lot of homework which I have to fit between working. Some days I wish I didn't have to work, but then how would I finance my fabric addiction? I love it and am very proud of what I have achieved in a relatively short time.

My first real quilt was made for my daughter, who is now a deck officer in the RFA. It's called Mermaid and was made with love for her, as she just adores the sea. When home on leave, she once went through my stash approximating its worth. Sadly, it's around the £3000.00 mark but I still add to it. I do have favourite designers and Amy Butler is just one of them. Sometimes I buy fabric which I know I shall never cut into. Where can I find help..?!

Currently I quilt in the dining room, however, for my birthday, I shall be the very proud owner of a wonderful quilting cabin, designed and built by my partner - at last somewhere to display all my fabrics! To me sewing takes me to a happy place, a place of quiet and total concentration on my work. I love learning new techniques and my tutor, Linda, is keen on teaching, so a match made in heaven. If I am interrupted, even by one of my cats who want my attention, I can get quite anxious and yearn to be back with my machine. Old Jones is still with me but has been updated by a wonderful all singing all dancing Janome. Quilting, and learning to use a machine has brought me happiness. The look on friends' faces when I gift them a piece of work is reward over and over. Quilts will outlast me, so I feel I am bequeathing parts of me to all my good friends who in turn think of me whenever they use them. What better gift or legacy can I give my daughter than to pass on my newly found skill set in order for her to pass onto her daughters one day?

My wish for a would-be quilter is to have a go. No matter what you make, or how long it takes, just know that your piece of art will probably outlive you. What better way to leave your mark on our world than with art. Consider making for charities too. Lots of newly born pre term babies love laying on the warmth of a quilt, as do rescue dogs and cats, so please think of them too. One piece of advice I wish someone had said to me: 'Buy fabric with a project in mind, not just cos you like it!' I have so much fabric, I wouldn't get through it if I quilted for another 60 years. Be warned, it is addictive! A.C.

Summer Porch from Eleanor Burns 'Quilting through the Seasons',
quilting by Janet McElroy. J.A.

The Northumberland Quilters

Dear Reader,

I'm a wife and mother of 3 grown up children and 6 stepchildren, with 6 grandkids and 3 more on the way. And I love quilting. I live in a small port town on the north east coast in Northumberland, which has high unemployment and not a lot going for it in general. I've been quilting for about 10 years and the first ever quilt I made was for my eldest granddaughter's cot. It was a steep learning curve as I didn't know what I was doing. I went to college and did a P&Q course to learn a bit more.

I suppose I started because I wanted to learn a new skill and make something that could be used and passed down through the years. It's very therapeutic to sit and sew bits of fabric together that don't look like anything at the start but end up looking beautiful and intricate. I recently finished the top of a hexagon quilt for another granddaughter, which contains over 800 x 1.25 hexies that I took all over the place. People were often amazed at the neatness of my stitches, the size of the hexagons and the design of it.

Unless I'm hand piecing, I do most of my quilting in my craft room, I hope none of the kids want to move back home! I have all the comforts – PC, TV, DVD player, CD player – and my fabric stash. It's a bit of a mess, but it's MY mess and I love it...organised chaos you might say. My granddaughter often keeps me company in there when she stays over, but the rest of the time I have Bon Jovi blasting away, or music from the 1970s, which relaxes me.

Probably the main reason I quilt is to pass on something that will hopefully become a treasured heirloom. There are so many different designs and new ones being brought out every day, it seems. If only I were rich and could buy all the fabric to make them all.

My sincere wish for the future is for this old tradition to be carried on. So many are forgotten about and it's a shame that they aren't passed down through the generations. I'll certainly be teaching my grandkids the art of patchwork and quilting and will hope that they carry it to teach THEIR children when I'm long gone. J. E.

Liberty, silk wadding – a luxurious quilt which set my path as a maker of quilts
An absolute joy from the first stitch to the last. K.J.

My hexie quilt. J.E.

The Nottinghamshire Quilters

Dear Reader,

I am a mother of 4 amazing children and although I am from a small town in Nottinghamshire, I live in the Middle East. I have to admit it, I'm a fabric'o'holic! I mean what's not to like, all those pretty patterns and yummy prints?

I was lucky enough to get a sewing machine for my birthday when I was a teen and made all sorts…cushions, bags and other little projects. Then a few years ago, I saw a quilt. It was beautiful and I wanted one. Being thrifty and completely mad, I thought 'I can make that!' Now we're not talking a sweet little nine patch, or easy squares, this quilt had hexagons. What was I thinking? I had no clue what I was doing, so obviously made it even harder by adding a bit of appliqué.

I set my machine up on a little table in front of an arm chair. (Long story, but the rabbit had chewed through the foot pedal cable and it was now about two foot long). Then I just went for it. Now you have to realize this is before I did any research or any classes. My little Singer hadn't even been cleaned or serviced, as I didn't know you needed to. I finished that quilt top and it was magnificent, as long as you just looked at the top and not underneath. Funnily enough, I was confident of taking on the top, but the thought of quilting just scared me to death, so I sent it off to be quilted. I must say it came back a bit of a masterpiece.

Since that first quilt I've been hooked. I find quilting so calming. I can be as creative as I want, I can use all my beautiful fabric that used to just sit in a cupboard for me to admire. I like the preciseness of quilting, but also the fact that you don't have to follow the rules and can try new things. Even if you were to learn a new technique every week, you'd still be learning new things in years to come. The possibilities are endless; a very dear friend introduced me to spray baste and I've never looked back! In fact, I think my favorite part is the quilting and binding; that sense of achievement as you're finishing yet another project. I love making quilts for friends and family, I see them as little fabric hugs from overseas.

If you have even a little spark of interest in sewing, give it a go. Now I'm not talking hexagons and appliqué, that's just crazy talk, but maybe a little lap quilt to get you started, I promise, you too will be addicted! I love quilting, I put my music on loud and sew. If the music is good, I sometimes have to get up and have a jig around, just to celebrate how great quilting makes me feel.

Don't think you have to be a grandma to quilt, although it's ok if you are, obviously! My best friend and I like to think of ourselves as quilt rebels, pushing the boundaries and experimenting. We quilt on the edge.... Well a quarter inch from it!!!! L.M.

M.B.

The Oxfordshire Quilters

Dear Reader,

I am a widow of 18 months and a mum to three grown-ups. For 28 years I have lived in my village, the longest time I have ever stayed in one place.

I am never happy unless I am making something, anything. I am relatively new to quilting, only starting in January 2015. After packing up my husbands' clothes, they sat in their bags for almost a year, because I didn't know what to do with them. Then one day I saw a quilt someone had made, and fell in love. I unpacked all of his shirts, cut them up and made my first quilt. A 'quilt as you go' disappearing nine patch. Quite a bit of 'unsewing' or reverse stitching, was done. It's not perfect, but it's perfectly perfect for me. I then went on to make three more quilts from his old clothes for my children. By then I was well and truly hooked and 'the rest', as they say, 'is history'. Like many people, I have a long list of 'would like to' makes and a few works in progress.

I enjoy the creative process of cutting up pieces of fabric and then sewing them all back together to make something entirely new. I must say that hunting down the right fabric is enjoyable too. Although sometimes my purse doesn't think so. I also love painting my own fabrics, which will eventually be cut up and sewn back together into wall hangings.

At the moment I sew at my dining table and sandwich quilts on my living room floor, where it is a constant battle with the cats as to who owns the floor. I have an Arty [painty] studio in my attic and am thinking of ways to get a large table up there, so I can move everything into one place and do not have to keep packing everything away. As a bit of an insomniac, you can find me sewing at any time of the day or night.

I have made many friends through my new 'addiction', both online and in person. They all offer wonderful words of advice and lots of encouragement when things don't quite go to plan.

My daughter loves choosing fabrics with me, but I have yet to persuade her to try her hand at sewing. In truth, she is a wee bit frightened of the sewing machine. But we will get there eventually. I am hoping that she will get the sewing bug and then in turn pass it on to her children. Trying to convince my sons is another matter entirely.

I love it, when I finish a project, whether simple or complicated, stand back and think 'Wow. I made that'. L.M.

I love the simplicity of this block. It's called 'the ten minute quilt block' and that's about right. K.S.

A Shropshire Quilter

Dear Reader,

I live in a very old small town, surrounded by beautiful countryside. I was a teacher for 39 years and am now the owner of a small business teaching sewing. I have only very recently discovered the delights of patchwork and quilting. My daughter decided that she would like to make a quilt. With the help of a friend I taught her how, before I had even had a go myself! We kept things simple using large squares and she chose all the fabrics to make a statement about herself. The backing was chosen as deer are her favourite Christmas symbol and she will be binding the quilt with the feather fabric because she wants to be free as a bird and travel the world.

I wanted to be able to teach patchwork and quilting, so I made a small lap quilt for my neighbours' daughter's 18th birthday. I discovered "just doing it" is a great teacher! It is strip pieced and designed to remind her of home. Blue is her favourite colour and the buttons represent her time helping me at my shop. The fabrics were chosen to remind her of flowers in the garden, dreams, making cups of tea for everyone, her butterfly brooch that her sister bought, blowing dandelion clocks when walking the dog, the birds they kept, going to the zoo etc. Yet at this point I still wasn't hooked.

I didn't decide that I actually liked quilting until after my dad died. A visit to "The Festival of Quilts" this summer, to find out what all the fuss was about, provided me with the inspiration to create something in his memory. I am making a quilt which hopefully conveys the sadness of losing my dad and things about him and his life. The black is the hole he left behind, purple the inspiration to join the Quilters Guild, blue represents his love of fishing and his garden ponds, green for the stripes on the lawn, growing vegetables and he was a greengrocer, yellow for his humour, orange for the koi carp and goldfish, red for the tomatoes he grew, the strawberries and red apples he sold. The quilt is also designed to be educational, as my dad taught a lot of people to fish and how to look after their ponds. Hence it is a colour wheel, to help people with colour choices. The final design will be that of a star, because he is my star in heaven and deeply missed by everyone … despite the fact that he could be very grumpy!

Quilting has enabled me to have a focus, which has helped distract me from the grief of losing my dad. It has given me purpose and helped to put joy back into my life. I would advise anyone thinking of taking up this fascinating and very diverse hobby to "just do it". Start small and keep it simple in the beginning. Discover your own style, likes and preferences, and have the courage to break the rules by doing it your way! I like the idea of telling a story, you may like a different approach. There are lots and lots of lovely sewers out there, all happy to give advice and help. It is a very friendly and sociable community. Remember that if we can do it, so can you! H.D.

Kate's Quilt and my first quilt

The Somerset Quilters

Dear Reader,

I live in the South West, with plenty of inspiration from the lovely landscapes all around us. I have sewn and embroidered from the age of 6 or 7, but only made my first quilt at college in the 70s. It was hand stitched, made of offcuts of all my projects, corduroy and cotton, silk and acrylic, and stuffed with cut up tights, lined with wadded nylon from a bedspread. Ugh. It was bright and warm and not very well made.

But as freedom from parenthood grew, I made more. Now I have the privilege of sewing them for grand babies of family and friends. I still use the sewing machine I had when my first child was born, but I sew in a cabin vacated as his workshop, by my son when he left home. I truly love the time I spend "in me shed".

The warmth and comradeship of patchworkers and quilters makes me feel part of a vast community, and makes me smile. My 97 year old mum has a little group of ladies who raise money for charity with her, making patchwork quilts: one makes the tea, one cuts out, one tells them what to do but has no experience, and they enjoy their afternoons chatting and working.

My wish is that everyone can find a niche in the world where they are important and contribute like this. M. A.

For my nephew. N.A.

The Staffordshire Quilters

Dear Reader,

I am a wife and a mother of four children and four dogs! I've spent my whole life in the West Midlands. I started quilting just over 18 months ago, after attending a local craft group and my first quilt was a massive learning curve.

I mainly started quilting to keep busy. As a depression and anxiety sufferer, I found having a quilt to focus on helped keep the worries at bay. I have made some wonderful friends and found so many other people that sew to soothe. I find the time spent choosing a pattern, fabrics and planning, really focuses you and stops the many distractions of every day. I may not be the best, but I love giving them to friends and family and seeing the versatile ways in which they are used, from the warmth on a sofa, to a play den for my nieces and nephews. Happy faces are the best pick you up.

I am lucky enough to have a whole room for my craft collection, and my husband refers to it as my happy place. I find that I can spend hours in there, just relaxing and sewing as much or as little as I want. I find that the music of my sewing machine is so calming and I enjoy watching a new project grow. I quilt when everyone else is asleep and I love the late night sessions that leave me watching the dawn break without even knowing it is a new day.

For anyone who is just thinking about quilting and looks at all the stunning quilts others have made thinking 'I could never do that', I'd say, don't get hung up, quilting is such a benefit, for peace of mind and soul and comfort to others. I feel that it has given me more confidence and with every new project the self-doubt fades. When finished, whether that is quickly or over a length of time, seeing the quilt that you have completed is such a sense of achievement. There is so much you can learn and there is no such thing as a mistake, every quilt is unique and is there to be loved.
L.S.

My first quilt, for my granddaughter. Just retired, newbie quilter .C.E.

A Suffolk Quilter

Dear Reader,

I live in Britain's largest container port, but love the fact that I'm minutes from quiet hamlets and villages on the coast or in the countryside. Needlework was my mother's holiday relaxation after a busy job and five children to bring up. Today I still treasure a log cabin quilt designed using our childhood dresses. It fills me with memories, but I had never thought of tackling a quilt. It was only before my retirement as a teacher, a textile loving friend encouraged me to be creative, I started on a basic quilting course and soon had the bug! Everyone else completed a flower design which was so not me, so I adapted it to be based on beach huts. Over the next 16 months I created and made a wedding quilt for my daughter. Developing appliqué, machine and hand quilting skills led me to produce an Irish Chain quilt, with hearts pattern. It became the wedding present money could not buy, with a border incorporating staves of the wedding music, as both are keen musicians. I vowed never to do a king size quilt again, but within a month, started another one using up all the leftovers for my husband and myself.

I love the creating and the wow when I have achieved, whilst the process is a comfort in both relaxation, yet learning new and exciting things. Overcoming those nitty problems is such a learning curve and I pick friends' brains if stuck before coming up with a solution I can cope with and has my individual twist on it.

Now I have different quilted projects on the go so I can pick up whatever the mood takes me, from bags and Ipod cases to massive king size quilts, which have all been produced in the four years I have been quilting with serious attitude! I recently converted my daughter's old bedroom to be my quilting room. My forty year old machine takes pride of place and still does admirable service.

I love going out with my textile friend, looking at others work and being inspired from those professional and those just starting. To the beginner I say enjoy yourself and don't get stressed when it has not quite gone as planned. Errors often only glare at you, not others, so don't focus on them, but be proud of what you have done. Yes there are always "targets for improvement" but I know I did my best at the time of making and no less love was incorporated with every stitch.

I know others are more gifted and sew neater, or have better colour sense, but in the end I am still learning and am progressing. Quilting is about reflecting my God given urge to create and be fulfilled by producing something that is made with love and to be loved, as I give something of myself and God to another, because they deserve it in my eyes. J.M.

Wedding scraps quilt.

The Surrey Quilters

Dear Reader,

I am an American girl who in my teens moved to the UK with my family. I am from a great make do and mend family, where every bit of wood, clothing, food was used up. My mother was a fantastic seamstress, professionally trained, and the majority of my early clothes were made by her. So from an early age I was on a sewing machine, making dolls clothes, Christmas ornaments and all sorts of textile goodies.

Like with most people, my focus wandered growing up. I painted, I photographed and sewing drifted away for many years. It really wasn't until I started to visit my sister-in-law that the quilting bug returned. The first quilt I made from start to finish was from scraps of fabric my mum had kept after making my baby clothes. The memories were so strong I couldn't bear to part with them and thought how wonderful it would be to make a keepsake from them. My mum has since passed away, and I swear I can still 'smell' her in those bits of cloth. It's the loveliest thing to wrap myself up in that first quilt, as I get a big hug from mum.

Besides the emotional connection, I find a quilt extremely satisfying to work on and complete. It's like a giant puzzle, with hundreds of ways to work it out. I can spend hours just playing with fabrics, to see which ones go together in my mind. Once at the quilting phase, I find great pleasure knowing the dark winter nights are filled not with TV or the web, but I actually have a product to show for it. I hate the feeling of wasted time – time is short enough as it is.

At the moment, quilting has taken over my home and well, threads are EVERYWHERE. There is a plastic box in every room with various sewing projects and spools. But plans are in place, and I hope to have a space outside next year – soon I can be surrounded by space and my fabrics. Any time is a good quilting time, although it does tend to be during my little one's nap times or nursery, which means short bursts of activity. She's grown up to the sounds of the hum of the machine and often plays nicely by my side.

Quilting offers me the challenge to find a new pleasing pattern, to immerse myself in a creative world, and focus on a project that is both practical and beautiful. I've made some wonderful friends through quilting that share the crafting spirit and help to inspire me to think beyond my four walls. I spend some of my time now helping others learn the basics to quilting and crafting. I find it's the joy to create something new and unique, and the pride that comes with this accomplishment. It is so satisfying it becomes infectious and soon your friends end up joining in too! What better way to enjoy one's friendship than nattering, spending time together and creating something lasting from our friendship. M.L.

First quilt for my mum, who is 90 this year. J.C.

The Sussex Quilters

Dear Reader,

I'm a wife, mother and grandmother and sometime have so many hats on I don't have time just to be me.... and that is where patchwork and quilting has come in. I am gradually reclaiming time to be me – the me that now wants to sew for pleasure. Allegedly retired, I still have a few things that take up my time, so I have more ideas of things to make than will actually come to fruition… but at least I will never run out of things to do.

I've always loved looking at patchwork quilts. I'm fascinated by the patterns that can be created by squares and triangles in fabrics. I even drove to the centre of Detroit to see an exhibition once – thank goodness everyone else stayed out of my way when I was lane changing.

When my sewing machine 'died' a couple of years ago, I was recommended to use a local fabric shop that had a franchise for a particular brand. The displays and fabric hooked me and I enrolled for a course to make a table runner. While checking their on-line diary, I noticed that one day a month was dedicated to making quilts for the 'Project Linus' charity. The store donated fabric and anyone could turn up and sew – bliss. As my grandson was given a Project Linus quilt when he was in hospital with meningitis, I was hooked and the rest as they say is history.

I'm still making my first proper quilt – a double bed size, for a friend who got married 3 months ago. I enjoy the charitable aspects that I can be involved in like Project Linus, and other 'Helping Hands' projects are in progress too. I have also made smaller items like mug rugs and tissue holders for church sales. For me, it is a way of giving, using my time and talents.

Although I am happy with my own company, I have recently joined a local group and relish the opportunity to sit and sew with others. The buzz of chatter and seeing everyone's projects, encourages me on to finish mine. There is great camaraderie among quilters and my UKQU Facebook family of quilters offer great advice, hints and tips, and support each other through triumphs and disasters – a modern version of village life. I wouldn't be without them. T.C.

'Harriet Tubman' Quilt L.T.

A Warwickshire Quilter

Dear Reader,

I am a married mum of three, but only one at home, and I live in a village in rural South Warwickshire, just three miles from where I was born. I help my husband with his business and look after our nine year old daughter and two labrador dogs. I would like to say that I learnt to sew at my mother's knee, or even my grandmother's knee, but unfortunately, I come from a long line of non-sewers! However, I did learn to sew at high school and had a very helpful neighbour, who would let me use her machine and help me out if I got stuck. Years ago, I used to dressmake, but, in my dreams, I would have been a pioneer on the trail across the USA, making quilts to brighten our log cabin!

Hence my whole life goal of being a quilter, but it did not actually happen until I was in my forties. A friend expressed an interest in quilting too, so we took a beginner's nine patch day course, about seven years ago, and I've quilted ever since. I have moved on from simple nine patch to more complicated blocks, foundation piecing and now just trying to have a go at art quilts. I upgraded my 1980s sewing machine to an all singing one about 18 months ago and also, with the departure from home of our grown up children, managed to acquire the smallest bedroom as a sewing room.

I think first and foremost all quilters love fabric. It does really become an obsession and you start to acquire much more fabric than you could possibly sew in a year or two. However, a room filled with lovely fabric is a very calming space and I sometimes just go into the sewing room and do nothing much, just look at everything! Once you start a project, you can pull out different fabrics, decide if they go together, decide what you might make, who for, or where it will go in the house. Sometimes find a fabric that's just perfect that you did not even know you had! At the end you can sit back and think, 'that's beautiful and I made that'. That's very satisfying. Also, the fact that I am carrying out a traditional craft is very important. I often imagine my work being seen by my descendants and them wondering what 'three times great granny' was like to have made this quilt.

A quilting journey is an ever changing one, you develop your ideas and skills, taking on a new project, maybe just a bit a harder than the last one, or maybe completely out of your comfort zone, and then get the thrill of

70

accomplishment when it's all done and being used. The other major influence that keeps me at it, is that my nine year old daughter looks likely to be a sewer too and so now we fabric shop and go into the sewing room together and I just love the idea that she will grow up to sew and I will have taught her. M.B.

This is why I quilt.
I like to think that in 100 years time, someone will look at this quilt
and wonder about the person who made it and the people who received it.

The Wiltshire Quilters

Dear Reader,

I have always had a love of patch work quilts since my child hood. I never had a quilt but loved the look of them, always noticing them in American movies, and how homely they made a room look. It was much later in my life that I became an owner of a real handmade patch work quilt. I spent many nights staying over at my best friend's house, where she had a quilt that was made by her aunt, it was various shades of purple and cream and I adored it. Every visit I would admire it and have the pleasure of burying myself under it for our movie nights, with munchies and wine. Some of the most treasured memories I hold.

It was in October 2009 I received a phone call from another friend to inform me that my beautiful friend had passed away, she was only 30 and suffered a massive heart attack. That moment in my life, my world stopped, she was the closest friend I'd ever had and life without her beauty and energy for life, seemed unbearable. My friend's parents very kindly passed the quilt to me, as my friend had told them I adored it. It became my most treasured possession, it gave me comfort in my grief and made my friend feel close. I entered a period of very deep depression, my only comfort was in the quilt I inherited. It took me quite some time to find a path to walk where my friend would not be by my side. The emptiness and loss felt so huge, I did not know where to start filling the void losing her had left.

I went to my first quilting class 2 years later, and started with my first project, I decided not to start small, and went straight in with a double sized quilt. I was doing it all by hand and it consumed all my energy. I found it a great release from my depression and loneliness. My first quilt took me 5 months to build and my friend was my inspiration, I used various star blocks. I gifted that quilt to my father. Since then I have made several other double quilts and gifted them to friends and family, and for each and every one, my friend is my inspiration.

I also have a love of making quilted bags, and have quite a collection of them now, they are my go to quick project. I have found peace with my grief in quilting and on my darkest days, I lose myself in making something special. I have learnt that something handmade can be of great comfort to people for many reasons, and I plan to make fidget quilts for dementia sufferers and small items like lavender bags for elderly people who live alone. There are so many good causes out there, where peace and happiness can be brought into lives with something that is a pleasure to make. My friends quilt still takes pride of place on my bed and brings me so much comfort, every day I feel her influence in my life. As a sufferer of depression, learning to quilt saved my life. L.M.

For my grandson. L.C.

A Worcestershire Quilter

Dear Reader,

I started patchwork classes 15 years ago, only because I had bought a template and fabric in the USA some 10 years before and couldn't make head nor tale of the instructions. My love for this crazy hobby took hold immediately and I joined a group in Wadebridge. It has been a lifeline for me as I didn't have any family or friends in Cornwall at that time and the comradeship and friendship I found has been constant since that time. I made quilts for all the family and always enjoyed the challenges that starting a new pattern would bring.

Last year, my husband was very ill and airlifted to hospital, again this wonderful hobby was there for me. During the long hours he slept, I stitched and it brought wonderful conversations from staff and visitors in the hospital.

We decided to move to be nearer the family and once again I am in a new area and yes, the family are all nearer, but again I miss my friends from Cornwall and yet again, it is quilting that picks me up and gives me new acquaintances that are becoming friends and another new group, with like-minded people, who are making me welcome.

Last year I became a member of UK Quilters United through Facebook and this group, no it's more than a group, this "family" support each other through the good times and the bad ones, another lifeline through the lonely first weeks in a new area.

My new home is being renovated and my sewing room will be on the first floor in our bungalow. I am able to plan it from the start, which is very exciting - do I have my work desks round the edge, or one big one in the middle, such a big decision. I like to have soothing background music on while I sew, and a plentiful supply of coffee, which he himself usually supplies.

My advice to any new quilters is not to rush into anything …at the moment, I am making 30 small bags for my teacher daughter, 2 slipper bags for granddaughters, bunting for a friends village, block of fabric to appliqué with leaves on for a group quilt and goodness knows how many projects I have of my own on the go… but to always enjoy your project.

Good luck and happy stitching! B.A.

For Rev

The Northern Irish Quilters

Dear Reader,

We are a pair of quilters. It's her fault! I am a workaholic, a lecturer and nurse, she is a translator and nurse. We both approached life at a hundred miles an hour, chasing careers and bringing up children. Then I had to have major, life-saving surgery at 45. I still attempted to work hard, ambition being the devil on my shoulder. One day she popped round to show me her new hobby, she was making a quilt for her teenage son, out of his dad's old pyjamas. I thought "If she can make one, then so can I". And so it began!

We live beside the River Bann in an area that has a strong tradition of stitching on the fine cotton that was produced in the country's flax mills. Our town is overlooked by a large, old manor house called "The Clothworker's Building". We embrace this tradition and consider ourselves to be modern cloth workers, using patches of cotton fabric to make colourful quilts.

We have created a sewing studio in my attic. Our stash is ever growing, but she justifies it by saying its good insulation! I prefer squares, she stitches triangles; she measures everything to the nearest mm, while I eyeball everything, improvising as I go along. Our mascot is her 9 year old daughter, who is constantly by our side. She holds the title of "Keeper of the buttons" and earns her keep picking up pins with her magnetic wand.

We sew every Saturday. Her daughter calls it "cake day" because in between the chain piecing and 'unsewing', we all drink tea and eat cake, a different one each week. We have made wedding quilts, baby quilts and many lap quilts for our families, but we have a quilting secret!

Quilting started as therapy for me, stopping me from working constantly, but we quickly realised that a quilt could provide therapy for others. So we are passionate about creating sensory quilts for those with learning disabilities, wee pocket sized ones that children can take from home to their special school or tiny quilts for premature babies in our local NICU. We design person centred fidget quilts for older people that have dementia care and have produced quilts for cancer patients. We have seen older people admitted to our local hospital who bring comforting blankets from home and realise the benefit of a photo memory quilt, so that patients can be surrounded by their loved ones while they are recovering, or even in their last days.

So, reader, that's our future, serving our local community the best way we know how. P.R. and C.H.

My First Quilt: McCullough's 'Apple Jack'.

For my daughter's best friend on the occasion of the birth of her first born. Made with fabric designed by Tim and Beck for Moda entitled 'Apple Jack,' inspired by his parents who are both primary school teachers. I thought, at the time, an apple for the teacher.

The quilt was named before the baby was born, so I was delighted when he was called Jack Herbie, the parents had no inkling about the fabric I used to make their quilt.

They are expecting their second child any minute and their latest quilt has been named, so we will see…P.R.

The Scottish Quilters

Dear Reader,

I am the mother of two grown-up daughters, grandmother to one granddaughter, and live with my husband of 45 years, and our cat, in the country close to the north coast of Scotland.

My first quilt was EPP hexagons for a cot quilt more than 40 years ago. Children, other crafts and work distracted me from quilting until 2001, when our local gallery had an exhibition of quilts. This coincided with our local college starting a night school class for quilting.

Since then, my passion and obsession has only increased! During the last few years of my working life, my few hours each week spent quilting saved my sanity. Now that I am retired, I am fortunate to be able to spend much of my time pursuing my obsession.

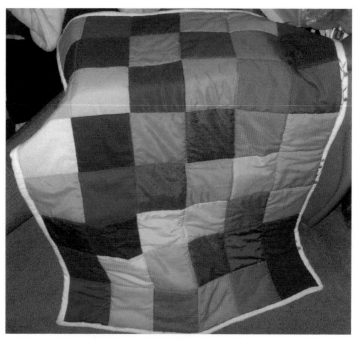

I love my first quilt. When I have children
this will be their play mat as it is lovely and thick. K.M.

Our spare bedroom becomes my sewing space for much of the year, and hardly a day passes when I don't spend some time there. I get enormous pleasure from working with beautiful fabrics, to create items which others appreciate, whether large or small projects.

My quilting has introduced me to people at home and around the world, who share my passion, people I now consider to be friends. The quilting community is very much a positive, sharing, supportive community. Long may that continue and expand. I.M.

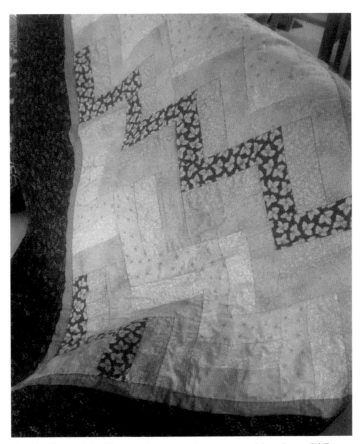

Aprils Cozy. My first quilt, made for my granddaughter. T.D.

The North Wales Quilters

Dear Reader,

I am a wife, mummy to a 4 year old and a 7 month old and I'm expecting our third little one. I am also mummy to 2 black labs. We all live on a beautiful island just off the Welsh coast.

I first had a go at hand quilting when I was just 10 years old and didn't really touch it again until I went to university, 8 years later. I am mostly self-taught, via the wonderful world of the internet and a few books. I have also attended several classes over the years, to help perfect my techniques.

Quilting for me is a little bit of 'me' time after the kids are in bed. I am very lucky and have a room dedicated to my quilting, so I don't have to put everything away at the end of a session. I enjoy watching old films whilst I quilt – 'Some Like It Hot' is one of my all-time favourites. I have recently been brought a quilting frame and new mid arm machine by my fabulous hubby. I look forward to getting to grips with my frame and what I am able to quilt on my finished quilt tops.

One of the main reasons for quilting, apart from the therapeutic side of it, is to be able to pass on quilts to my children and maybe their children. I love the idea of a piece of me being passed on to my future generations. I am also passionate to keep this beautiful art going, as it has been lost over the generations, with mothers no longer teaching their daughters and sons how to quilt / sew.

My wish for a would-be quilter is 'don't over criticise your work, it is beautiful and unique to you, and above all…enjoy it'! G.R.

Blooming Miracle. S.W.

The South Wales Quilters

Dear Reader,

I am 66 and am married with two children. I live near Tenby in Pembrokeshire, with my husband and 91 year old mother. I have been involved with art and crafts in one form or another all my life. One of my earliest memories is of my grandmother doing raffia work, sitting in the kitchen with the raffia hanging on the wall beside her. My mother said I spent a lot of my time leaning against her knee as she worked. As she died when I was four and I can still see it in my mind's eye, it must have meant a lot to me. Then, as I got older, I remember an aunt embroidering and my mother making rag rugs and knitting. These things were not done as hobbies but were a necessary part of daily life. So it is hardly surprising I got the making bug early.

I had many happy years teaching art to young children, but always, always, somehow I found a place in my life for my own art or craft. Then one day I decided to make an appliqué hanging, using the children's handprints, realised there were skills I needed to know, went along to my local patchwork group and was hooked. For the first time I no longer had to fight paint or glaze which never gave me the colour I wanted; there, in front of me, were spectrums of colour, patterned, polychromatic, kaleidoscopic, marbled batiks and fabric with gold on! Then the patterns one can cut them into, from traditional to modern to make it up as you go along, the possibilities are endless. Then appliqué through to art quilts and experimenting with the fabric itself; and all of this in the company of other like-minded people.

I am sure it comes as no surprise to any patchwork and quilter that research done at Glasgow University has shown that patchwork is one of the best hobbies you can do for mental and emotional health. From the dreaded maths needed for sashing and borders, through to sharing life's big (and not so big) problems with sympathetic friends, there is nothing like the quilting group, all wearing their metaphorical red hats.

Patchwork became so central to my life that when the opportunity arose I bought a shop. I am past retirement age, but keep giving myself one more year. What would I do without all the friends I have made, all the fabric I'm allowed to buy, all the classes I design and run? For many of my ladies it is a lifeline, a day they can give to themselves, away from family problems and responsibilities, with the only stress being matching fabric and 'who's turn is it to make the tea'.

So for now, one more year; and I have a couple of new ideas for quilts. G.S.

P.S. If I live as long as my mother, I may even make all the quilts I have running around inside my head. On the other hand, probably not!

'Double Wedding Ring' for my parents golden wedding anniversary.
It took 3 years of planning, was horrendous and I'll never do one so hard again! A.W.

The Belfast Quilters

Dear Reader,

I am now a widow, with two grown up children and three grandchildren, I live in Northern Ireland. I have been quilting twenty five years now and patchwork has become an addiction!

I had never heard of patchwork and I don't remember ever seeing it as a child. My father did embroidery and my mother sewed our clothes when I was young, so sewing ran in the family, so to speak. These were the days when sewing was taught in school and I loved my sewing classes.

As I grew older I was very much into embroidery and dressmaking. I worked in Further Education, and one day the principal stopped me along the corridor saying 'you do that sewing thing, will you take a ten week course?' After I had got over the shock, I said yes and built my lessons round embroidery, however whilst planning I discovered this thing called appliqué, patchwork and quilting and it looked nice, so a few practice attempts and sure I knew everything about patchwork!

At the same time I contacted the textile curator on another matter at Cultra, in Belfast and talk came round to quilts and she said 'do you want to see what we have in the archives?' Well, to say I died went to heaven and never have landed back on earth is no exaggeration!

I also discovered I knew nothing about quilting.

This was the start of my journey, very much self-taught. I have been very lucky, I continued to teach patchwork and still do. I have made so many friends and received so much help from complete strangers round the world via many yahoo groups I signed up to. Patchwork has encouraged me to extend my horizons, both in the mind and in travel, imagine a class in Spain! The dream is a quilt cruise in Alaska and yes, it is possible.

My family has many of my quilts. To think that someday future generations may be inspired, as I was, is comforting.

If you are reading this, then you are on the same journey. Enjoy it, embrace the challenges, decide what your work is going to be; is it going to be for exhibition purposes, (points matter) or is it to be used on a daily basis (maybe points won't matter). Remember, when you give a quilt it is no longer yours, what the recipient does with it may not be what you had in mind, enjoy giving the gift.

Finally, if someone says 'you do that quilting thing, will you teach it?'…
do it. I.R.

My first half square triangles quilt. P.M.

A Birmingham Quilter

Dear Reader,

I first started my interest in patchwork nearly 40 years ago, around the time of the American Bicentennial, but resources were thin on the ground in Birmingham at that time. When I had my first son, who has a learning disability, I was lucky enough to find adult education classes with a wonderful teacher. Oh, how this was a life saver!

And patchwork and quilting has been my comfort ever since. The groups I've joined and women I've met have been a tremendous source of support and have enabled me to reciprocate. The act of regularly meeting and sewing with a group of women of various ages and backgrounds seemed to connect directly to all the groups of women who did the same in the past and in other places. Something about having busy hands makes it easier to talk through the most difficult issues.

Increasingly, I have become more interested in getting closer to how our forebears worked, using scraps, sewing by hand and hand quilting all have a soothing rhythm to lose my troubles in.

Those of us involved in this wonderful craft are truly fortunate, we are able to share companionship, skills, fabric (of course), laughter (often), cake (invariably) and friendships that last a lifetime. C.W.

My first 'disappearing 9 patch' with hearts and flowers borders.

The Bristol Quilters

Dear Reader,

I live in Bristol. My children are now in their early 20's and I'm slowly getting used to not having them around all the time. I work full time in education and over the last few years my job has become more and more stressful and busy. A couple of years ago I decided to try to balance my life and work a bit more.

I always used to sew, knit, and crochet, even made cards and did some stained glass, but I've not really done any patchwork. I signed up for a 6 week evening course one September.....my plan was to ensure I had something other than work to focus on, as work was drifting into my own time too much.

I did a local course, made a quilt in six weeks and loved every minute of it. I showed it to my sister, who also works full time in an even more stressful job in social care. She loved the quilt and suddenly decided she was very keen, so we went on a workshop together and made a small mat. My sister was so pleased with it, she carried on and made it into a quilt!

Since then we have really enjoyed making patchwork, she has become fantastic at free machine quilting (FMQ) and made two quilts. I've made three quilts and various smaller things. We go out to different material shops and workshops together, planning days out to include lunch and various tea stops! It's great to spend time doing something enjoyable and lovely to spend time together doing these things.

We have stayed in a B&B with a quilting retreat twice now and are planning a third time. It's good fun, really good for stress management and we make some lovely things as we go along. Fabric shopping is great......on a forum someone called it a FARTing day (Fabric Acquisition Road Trip) ...so we often have FARTing days with lunch out!   D.D.

My first quilt. L.M.

The Cardiff Quilters

Dear Reader,

Do you fancy a bit of stitching? Do you like cake? If you answered yes to either or both, then please read on. I'm a 50 something (OK fast approaching the big 60) wife, mother, nanna etc. I was born and brought up in South Wales. I grew up sewing, knitting, crocheting, simply following what my mother and gran did. I have a lifelong love of creating, making gifts for friends and family. This stems from reading Little Women as a child and falling in love with the idea of making Christmas gifts for loved ones. My sister first introduced me to patchwork and quilting around 19 years ago. I was on long term sick leave and had become a little bored. My sister who had recently 'discovered' patchwork, brought me a Dresden Plate pattern to hand stitch. I was instantly hooked, and the rest, as they say, is history.

On a visit to my doctor, feeling a little down and sorry for myself, he suggested I get myself out and join some kind of group. He had no idea what he started for me that day. Over the next few years I joined a couple of quilting groups, the Quilters Guild and several on-line groups. In my local group I began by offering to help wash the cups up - always a good way to break the ice and make friends when you are a new girl. I know I am lucky that I have the confidence to go places on my own, and honestly, everyone was very welcoming and friendly, and I quickly became part of each group. I've been on group committees (something I thought I would never do). I've run trips and workshops, started a quilting blog, been involved in fabric/block swaps. I also realised that I had a passion for helping others to learn. I am an eternal learner myself and spend many a happy hour researching different patchwork and quilting techniques.

So, what have I got out of this hobby of mine? Fantastic friendships - I have made so many quilty friends over the years. Support - both creative and emotional as friendships have grown. Inspiration - meeting up with other like-minded quilters and seeing all their different ideas. Fun - I cannot begin to tell you just how much fun we have in our classes and groups. Cake - many quilters enjoy baking and we take advantage of every opportunity to celebrate with cake; birthdays, anniversaries, workshops....did you know cakes eaten at quilting events have zero calories, or did I dream that bit?

Finally, here is my piece of advice: Take one small step forward, join up, or, scary one now - start your own little group. Participate, get involved, you never know where it might lead. Just pick one little step and say hello to the wonderful world of quilters.

We are all waiting to welcome you. J. M.

In memory of Dad. H.R.

The Edinburgh Quilters

Dear Reader,

I am a 40 something single lady and I have a passion for quilting. I live in a small town in a beautiful part of Scotland and have been quilting for only five years. The first quilt I ever made was the Harriet Tubman Railroad Quilt, containing many different blocks and was a complete eye opener into patchwork and hand quilting in general. I then discovered that my meticulous nature had finally found a purpose, piecing was my ultimate destiny, and I loved it!

As I said, I am 40 and single and live at home with my parents. No, I am not a boring person with no life, but when I was 18 my father was diagnosed with Parkinson's disease and I was needed to stay at home to support the family. I then began to cross stitch at home in the evenings when I needed to keep my mind active. About 5 years ago, a friend told me about a craft club starting locally. Within weeks I found a new lease of life in the quilting class, and began to enjoy matching colours, especially different shades of purple. Now every member of my family owns a quilt hand made by me and they were all made with a lot of love and emotion.

Not only did I get the new lease of life from the enjoyment of quilting, but I made new friends as well, friends who have become close and extremely helpful over this last year. This has been a year of hell for myself, having spent most of the year in hospital. It then got worse when my aunt died in July, closely followed by my father in August. The first thing I headed for was my sewing machine and my quilting book and my plan for a new quilt to be made in their honour and perhaps raffled for a local charity.

Next stop the material shops and I'll have everything I need. J.B.

'Wonky log cabin', made for the local day centre bus. A.M.

Ollie, the first quilt I became emotionally attached to,
as it reminds me of Mum who has Alzheimer's. K.F.

A Liverpool Quilter

Dear Reader,

My journey into patchwork and quilting began in 2000. I had always fancied it, but my only knowledge was of the English paper piece hexagons and the idea of this left me cold. Visiting a friend, I was intrigued by the quilt she was making for her grandson from half square triangles. She showed me how to do these and I went home and searched through my bag of scrap fabrics, some from dress making some from curtain making and began making half square triangles. I had no idea how to put the things together, but working from the first square, I sort of worked out. Eventually I decided that I needed some help with this and found a local quilt group. They took me under their wing and I began to learn various techniques. I even put my first quilt into their little show. The quilting left a lot to be desired but I had enjoyed the process and was well and truly hooked.

A couple of years later we moved to the North West and I found another quilting group, Southport Quilters. Again, very welcoming and once again I began learning from other members and tutors. We had a talk from one of the members about quilts and slavery. The story was from a book called 'Hidden in Plain View'. I was totally enthralled by this story and bought the book. We have a daughter who lives in the USA and we visit each year. Of course high on the agenda a visit to quilt stores had become one of my must dos. On visiting a store I spotted a book by Eleanor Burns for making a sampler quilt of blocks supposedly used as a code for escaping slaves. The patterns were said to have directed them to the safety of the free northern states. Of course I bought the book and made the sampler quilt.

Telling a friend about my latest project, she asked if I would come and give a talk to her group. I only had my small sampler quilt to show and a few borrowed from other friends that were relevant to the talk. I enjoyed giving the talk and was asked to do another, so I then set to and made more quilts, each one a pattern block from the sampler quilt.

Sadly in 2008 my husband was diagnosed with Parkinson's and I felt helpless. But then a thought struck me. I could sort of help by giving my talks and raising money for Parkinson's research. And so began another interesting turn in my quilting story. I called my talk 'Fact or Fabrication', because the story of quilts actually being used to point the way or give direction to the fleeing slaves is a little far-fetched and in parts highly improbable. But it makes a good story and highlighted the plight of slaves. I have made about 16 quilts and for most of my talks my husband has come with me to help hold up the quilts, he's my Quilt Angel. I decided that my aim was to raise awareness of Parkinson's and to raise £2000. This I achieved last year and as my husband is no longer able to drive and my eyesight is not so good for driving at night, I have now given up on the talks.

I am still amazed that seeing my friend in Kent making half square triangles and teaching me how has led to not only my love of making quilts and hand quilting, but to opening a world of friends from up and down the country. So dear reader, pick up your needle and give it a go....there's no knowing where it might lead! P.M.

Simply Blue

A Manchester Quilter

Dear Reader,

I'm 54, have three sons and two very young grandsons. I live with my partner, my son and a daft dog. I work full time in a job that is stressful, hectic and extremely busy.

I started quilting about four years ago. My hubby had his hobby of flying aircraft and helicopters and I found myself sat doing nothing whilst he was off doing his thing. Knowing my love of crafts, he suggested getting his sewing machine out to let me get in some practice after years of no sewing. I started "messing around" and, before I knew it, I had made a block – fairly primitive, but neat, tidy and definitely a block. I then found myself buying a very basic sewing machine for myself. I also did my research and accidently discovered Craftsy online. The beautiful quilts and work on their site piqued my interest even further, so I paid to follow one of their Block of the Month courses and proceeded, over a few weeks, to make loads of lovely blocks. Then I became a nana and felt compelled to make my beloved grandson a small quilt. The rest is history.

Due to the stressful nature of my job, it is good to have something to do with my time which I find to be therapeutic. It is also addictive, a great de-stressor and just simply satisfying. Fortunately it doesn't affect my health conditions which are affected badly by knitting and embroidery (other crafts I used to do regularly). I've made so many new friends and gained so many new experiences just by being able to sew a straight seam. Who'd have thought it?

I've made a number of quilts for family members and friends over the last few years. I have also made a number for dog rescue charity auctions I am involved with. My proudest moment was when a lady from America bought a quilt I had made for a lot of money (for the charity). She later told me she had bought it for her dog but that it was too well made to let the dog have…a compliment indeed.

Whilst I don't have a specific room to quilt in, I live forever in hope. I currently quilt in a very small corner in what used to be my spare room until my youngest son decided to return home to live. Fortunately he spends time at his girlfriend's, so I get to quilt at these times, but space is really limited and I often find myself working on the corner of a table. I could definitely do with more space, especially with the amount of fabrics and patterns etc that seem to have moved in too! I could also do with the girlfriend wanting to spend a lot more time with my son!

I introduced my sister to quilting quite by accident. She admired some work I had done, so I suggested she take some of my fabric and a couple of my books. She went on to make four cushion covers which were lovely and has just gone on from there. She is far more organised than me though and will only ever have one quilt on the go – I've got three on the go currently. I have to have my Kindle on whilst sewing, but find I don't actually hear the music because I am so engrossed – perhaps I could save electricity by not having it on, but I don't feel as organised or enjoy it as much without the music. I find time flies by and several hours can just vanish without me realising.

I quilt first and foremost to keep myself busy. I have health conditions which mean I stiffen up badly. Quilting just keeps me moving. The satisfaction of completing a quilt is second to none. The compliments on a piece of work well done are worth every stitch that has been ripped out, every time I've burnt my fingers on the iron and every time my thread or needle has broken. I just feel so proud when I see it completed and I am very proud to call myself a quilter.

I hope any would be quilter would get at least half the stress relief I enjoy when quilting. A great starting place for advice, information and demonstrations of techniques is YouTube and it's free. Also the quilt shows are a great source of inspiration and they showcase the most beautiful quilts that we can all aspire to. D.M.

My first quilt and my latest quilt.

The North Yorkshire Quilters

Dear Reader,

I live in a beautiful part of England, on the edge of the north Yorkshire moors. My home is in the middle of a wood, by a river. It's shared with my husband and our three dogs.

I have only been quilting for three years, so am quite a newbie, but in that time it has become my passion and I quilt every day. Quilting has also taken over my social life as well. I am a member of three quilt groups and this has enabled me to meet some lovely people, who share their talent and skills.

Why quilt? Well, ill health has compelled me to give up so many things, but quilting is something anyone can do. I am lucky to have a sewing room, but it isn't a necessity, the corner of the table will do. A basic sewing machine and some cotton fabric is all you need to get going.

Rose Window J.M.

Making things for others is so satisfying … even each of my dogs has a handmade quilt! They say a quilt is a hug you can keep and every time someone uses it, they will think of you. In this way, you give a little of yourself in everything you make.

You can start quilting at any age and I just wish I had found this wonderful hobby when I was younger. It has opened up a whole new world to me. J.M.

Pineapple Blossom scrap busting my brights and colourfuls stash. R.E.

The South Yorkshire Quilters

Dear Reader,

I'm a busy wife and mum to grown up still at home children. I'm a newbie to quilting as I've only been doing it for 9 months but had been on the outskirts for a few years.

I was inspired by a Carol Shields novel called 'Happenstance' which ignited my desire to have a go...I just needed time.

Seeing a mystery challenge at the beginning of the year I thought why not! Not someone who was any good with a sewing machine, I was happy that this was hand sewing. English paper piecing, it resonated with my desire to preserve traditional skills and I want to hand quilt too.

Whatever stresses, problems or worries, when I start to quilt it's like a meditation. The repetitive stitching takes me away, soothing and calming jangled nerves. It's like being in a bubble...peace, calm and solitude...it doesn't matter where I am, it allows me to "be", recharging my batteries, away from business stresses.

I stitch anywhere and love sharing with others when asked. I've made friend with people across the globe by sharing my passion. How wonderful to see how quilting is diverse across cultures, yet retains the same basic aspects.

In the future, I hope that people will see the benefit of this simple tradition to produce fabulous, useful quilts, while breaking free from high tech pursuits, to keep alive a beautiful skill and maintain a personal pleasure and sense of wellbeing.

With quilting wishes. S.H.

J.S.

The East Yorkshire Quilters

Dear Reader,

I live in a seaside town and with my husband I run a small hotel. I have sewn all my life and got my own sewing machine at the age of 10. I regularly came home to a bundle of fabric and my mum asking me to make her a new dress for the next day! About seven years ago, she bought me a Janome 11000, it came with a quilting kit. I had never done any patchwork so ordered a book, 'Start Quilting' by Alex Anderson. I knew nothing about mixing colours and patterns and instead I ordered fabrics which I liked, but not necessarily went together. I made my first quilt and I was hooked!

My husband grew up with Susan Briscoe, a well-known quilter. As my interest grew I started asking more questions, until she said 'get a group together and I will come and teach'. We turned our large dining area at the hotel into a sewing room, Susan came for three days and we had a ball. The ladies loved it, I was rather taken back, but started to research interesting tutors. I organised a few more retreats and word spread. Susan ran a Sashiko retreat and Lilian Hedley booked on the course. After, she offered to teach too. Soon my database of quilters and tutors was growing beyond belief and I was organising workshops and retreats throughout our winter season, then spring and then a couple of summer weeks too, aiming to cover costs and provide much needed work in the quieter season for our staff.

My knowledge and skills improved as did my pile of UFOs (UnFinished Objects)! Like many, I would rather start a new top then quilt one. I began researching alternative quilting options. Two years ago, we imported our own ABM Innova longarm from the USA. Then we went out for a week of intensive training. America was truly AWESOME and we learnt so much. When we returned we had arranged to hold a charity quiltathon. By the time of the show we had quilted over 80 quilts. This led to the launch of 'Quilt Sandwich' – my longarm quilting service, but we had difficulty finding extra wide fabric, so I started to stock it and now sell over 120 different backing fabrics! I make memory quilts, organise workshops and retreats with tutors from the UK and abroad, am a longarm quilter, have an online shop and of course I'm a hotelier as well! I love to sew and I need a daily fix. I especially love to see customers' faces when they return to collect a quilt, after the longarm has worked its magic.

The world of patchwork and quilting has changed not only my life but my husband's too. We have made so many friends all over the world. Quilting has also taken over our business and our home, with stash and equipment & stock everywhere – but we love it. For anyone thinking about starting, don't be put off attending workshops and retreats because you're just a beginner. We all started there and in every session there are always mixed levels of abilities. Just give it a go! F.G.

'Sew A Row'. P.W.

A West Yorkshire Quilter

Dear Reader,

I live with my partner and two cats, Misty and Lucky. I started quilting about two years ago after giving up work due to cancer and other illnesses. I was a textile designer before having my children and as the years drifted away, my art did too.

I worked on some cross stitch designs while I was in hospital and found it took my mind to another place. When I came home, I gradually started doing embroidery, quilting, crochet and other crafts. It is so therapeutic and whenever I have been ill, I feel so much better for it.

I don't have a sewing room, but in the corner of my lounge are all my fabrics, books and other equipment, I do try to keep it organised. On an afternoon or evening, mostly evenings, I sew and embroider with either the TV on, or some music, and drift away...I really feel relaxed.

Quilting is so relaxing and exciting – you can't wait until you see the finished piece of work, then there is such a sense of elation. I would advise any person to do patchwork and quilting, even if they haven't sewn before, for both the experience of making beautiful artwork, and the therapeutic side of it. D.L.

For my grandson, due tomorrow.

THE QUILTED KINGDOM

UK Wall-hanging by AbbieAnne Searle

Instructions:

These instructions are for you to make your wall-hanging using a raw edge version of reverse appliqué. Your pattern will need to be enlarged to at least A1 for you to complete it. Please do not worry if the design looks too complicated, as you transfer your pattern to fabric, you will automatically adjust the detail line to suit yourself.

Requirements for A1 size:

1 x plain top fabric, cotton 24" x 34" (this will become your outline)
5 (or more) other fabrics 24" x 34" (1 x blue, 3 x green, 1 x brown)
Complimentary threads (variegated has been used in the example)
1 x wadding 26" x 36"
1 x Backing/binding 27" x 37"
Small sharp pointy scissors
A new machine needle, fabric marker, general sewing kit.

How to:

Transfer your design onto the right side of the top fabric, (light box or whatever technique suits you).
Lay your other fabrics on top of each other, right-sides up.
Place the design piece of fabric on the top of the pile.
Secure all the layers ready for machining (or hand stitching, tightly!)
Stitch the design through all of the layers using a very tight stitch, a zigzag or fancy stitch, we all have them and don't use them!
You may need to adjust your tension, please do not touch the bottom tension!!
It's the top that matters, we won't see the bottom.
Now cut away the layers of fabric from the top, between the stitching, being careful not to cut your stitching, so revealing the colours below.

When you're happy with the look of your design, cut away any excess fabric from the back.

Layer your backing/wadding/top, quilt in whatever style suits you.

Bind. There should be enough backing fabric to bring forward to bind or add a separate binding as suits you. Maybe add a border, it's endless.......

More detailed instructions for this technique are available in the book: 'Pile & Plunder, a form of Reverse Appliqué' by AbbieAnne Searle, available at www.abbieanne.com ISBN 978-095-7042-10-0 or call
Abbie on 07940133116

The Quilted Kingdom wall-hanging

The Quilted Kingdom: Pattern

Printed in Great Britain
by Amazon